Level 7 Performance

Level 7 Performance

The system to drive profits, employee involvement, and simplicity in the new world

Michael L. Goolden with Sandra L. Goolden

iUniverse, Inc.
New York Lincoln Shanghai

Level 7 Performance
The system to drive profits, employee involvement,
and simplicity in the new world

iUniverse books may be ordered through booksellers or by contacting:

iUniverse
2021 Pine Lake Road, Suite 100
Lincoln, NE 68512
www.iuniverse.com
1-800-Authors (1-800-288-4677)

Because of the dynamic nature of the Internet, any Web addresses or links contained in this book may have changed since publication and may no longer be valid.

The views expressed in this work are solely those of the author and do not necessarily reflect the views of the publisher, and the publisher hereby disclaims any responsibility for them.

ISBN: 978-0-595-44502-8 (pbk)
ISBN: 978-0-595-69856-1 (cloth)
ISBN: 978-0-595-88829-0 (ebk)

Printed in the United States of America

This book is dedicated to the Lord, my wife Pamela, my sons CJ and Joe, my daughter Sarah, my sister, Editor and content contributor Sandi Goolden, and all the friends, contributors and work associates who made this book possible with a special thanks to Lee & Carole Goolden, Rick Allen, Lawrence Waugh, John Norman, Mark Geene, Marc Isaacson, Brad Van Horn, John Kelley and Chuck Bokar.

Table of Contents

Section 1

Introduction: The New World Business Challenges 1

Section 2

Characteristics of Level 7 Companies and CEOs 7

Section 3

The Road to Level 7 11

Section 4

Basics of a Successful Level 7 System 15

Section 5

Key Business Measures for Your Business 29

Section 6

Reaching Level 7—Putting it All Together 43

Larry's Level 7 Story 49

R/x: Eighteen Prescriptions to Help Your Business Reach Level 7 67

Level 7 Performance Management System Nuts and Bolts 69

About the Authors 99

Introduction:
The New World Business Challenges

This book is a step-by-step guide to help you transform your business into a high level performer on a par with the world's best businesses—a new approach to performance management that we are calling "Level 7." This approach works independently or combined with the best of current performance thinking, such as Six Sigma or Malcolm Baldrige. Either way it will help your business move up to the next level and put in motion the steps to allow you to become a Level 7 leader in the new world.

Changes in the world are happening at an increasingly rapid pace. Faster business market and job employment cycles, accelerating technology and global competition, new regulatory control and terrorism are changing the world that you are working in by the minute. This new, sometimes confusing, and often decentralized environment means that you, as a business owner, manager, or employee, need to sharpen your reflexes and reactions if you want to excel. Tom Peters aptly lays out what the new business world looks like in his book <u>Re-imagine</u>:

What Was	What Is
Steep bureaucratic, with lots of "brass"	Flat, decentralized with little "brass"
A job for life—key word: "career"	A life full of jobs—key word: "projects"
Success-to-failure cycles last decades	Success-to-failure cycles last months

Technology supports change	Technology drives change
Employees	Talent
Technology helps link parts of the organization	The network is the organization
Every department uses IS/IT	Every department lives on the web
Every one labors under strict "need to know" rules	Every employee has access to know everything
We are proud of being close to the customer	We are proudly "at one" with our customer
"Silos" and "stovepipes"	One seamless enterprise
Depend on admin support "back at the ranch"	Carry a wireless "office" wherever you go
Get big fast	Get a clue
Passive Board of Directors	Pushy Board of Directors
Acquisitions: buying bulk	Acquisitions: buying innovation

Despite what is obviously a sea change, performance management until now has stayed mired in 1980s thinking and design. A Level 7 system allows you to position your business to make the most of this decentralized new world.

Many new decentralized forces have manifested themselves in our lives today. The Internet is one of the key drivers for the new global challenges. We are in a new phase for strategy and business performance. Many businesses and organizations have already recognized the power of these forces and have used them to unite and grow their businesses.

These Level 7 companies have used these forces in their favor to help retain employees and effectively fend off competitors. There are also examples of how these trends are allowing organizational networks from all over the world to unite and grow synergistically at the same time.

Changes in technology such as the proliferation of rapid Internet speeds, inexpensive hard drive memory, cellular Internet mobility and now Level 7 systems enable any company, large or small, to take advantage of what the successful "big boys" have had for years.... the opportunity to realize their organization's true potential. Leaders need relevant, real-time, accountable information with increasing frequency, while at the same time connecting their employee networks. Lacking this, management is ineffective at being proactive to market pressures in an appropriate and effective manner.

Level 7 systems provide your company with an opportunity to connect your people and your strategy with your daily tactical execution.

Very few companies bother to do this, although nearly every company can.

A recent study of companies by Marakon Associates found that on average, companies deliver only 63% of the financial performance predicted by their strategies.[1]

The companies that fared the best in the Marakon Associates study concentrated on planning and execution simultaneously, with clear links

---

1. Mankins, Michael C. and Richard Steele. "Turning Great Strategy Into Great Performance", Harvard Business Review OnPoint, Fall 2006, page 108 (originally published in 2005).

between these two formerly isolated processes. The performance gaps that the researchers found include strategy and performance disconnects, tactical execution and accountability disconnects, process, systems, communication and incentive disconnects.

Below is a visual look at what the researchers discovered about how businesses are falling short given these disconnects:

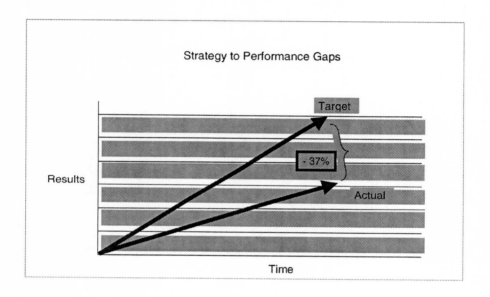

We have found a strong correlation between implementing Level 7 principles and double-digit results, as depicted in the following graph:

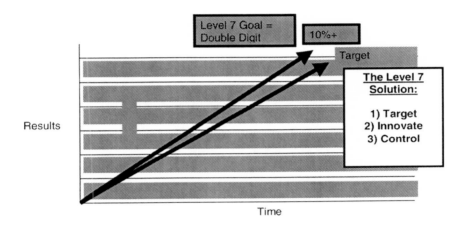

Reaching Level 7 will help you to strengthen control of your business priorities and show you how to tactically execute your priorities for improved results in the new business world. We will show you just what a Level 7 system can mean in terms of improved results in all areas of your business. Read on!

Section 2

Characteristics of Level 7 Companies and CEOs

Some companies have already made the transition to Level 7 principles by making the changes that are needed in order to adapt and prosper in the new decentralized world. In this section, we will show you what makes these performers stand out from the rest of the field.

As any student of Business 101 knows, all businesses require a viable product or service, attention to customers, and an existing or created market in order to succeed. Looking beyond this, we find that what has historically separated the mediocre performers from the world's highest ranked businesses are two major components: inspired, talented leadership, and thoughtful process management.

In addition to the two qualities that define the highest performers, there is now a third leg to the stool:

In the new decentralized world, before you can transform your business to its highest potential, Level 7, you need to have highly functional, responsive, and adaptable performance management systems in place.

The Marakon Associates study[2] we referenced earlier found that the high performers consistently used real-time performance management tracking systems to keep planning and implementation linked. This can be done for major projects and/or for the entire company.

By now, perhaps you're wondering: what exactly is performance management? *Business Performance Magazine,* an excellent performance publication, defines it as a set of management and analytic processes, supported by technology, that enables businesses to define strategic goals and then measure and manage performance against these goals. Core performance management processes include financial and operating planning, consolidating and reporting, business modeling, analysis, and monitoring of key performance indicators linked to strategy.

Level 7 business performance management when implemented correctly unites and connects the employees company-wide in an open system—teaching the entire company the same terminology and measurements of what success looks like. Level 7 systems increase the velocity of relevant information, at the same time creating visual community accountability.

Your company can now reach the standard set by these high-performing companies much more quickly than in years past.

In Level 7 companies, everyone in the organization understands what the priorities are. They know what success looks like. They are linked in an open system, yet still have accountability. The process starts with a Level 7 CEO or a project leader picking the key targets that measure suc-

---

2. IBID, pg 106.

cess. The Level 7 CEO always knows the status of his or her seven top key measures of success and the seven top projects driving them.

In our work with CEOs, they sometimes ask us why we are focused on seven key measures. Research has shown that seven continuous processes are the most that any one person's mind can process and handle at any given time. If you are juggling too many balls, you are bound to drop one or two and eventually all of them.

Throughout the book we use a proven simplification method of seven in several ways. Some of the Level 7 principles in this book are:

There are seven key business measures relative to all businesses and projects. This provides a common language and ease of communication for all participants within the open system.

The Level 7 scoring system, which provides a common method of relativity for comparing output.

The seven phases of any business. The first five phases have been documented for years; now businesses are experiencing phases 6 and 7 with the new technology and open decentralized world of networks.

We also provide you with a seven step framework to tie the system together. Several templates are available on our website at www.L7 pm.com for your use on your journey to Level 7.

The "Principles of Seven" outlined above are the basis for the success of the Level 7 system: simplification, and therefore, a short learning time.

Getting to Level 7 is the price of admission for a successful business in the new world. Your organization can do it—*if* you step out of old ways of thinking and move quickly and efficiently towards your goals using the right focus and the right tools. The Level 7 business will be the victor in the new world, and you can get there faster than you think. Section 3 will help you explore where your business is on the path to reaching Level 7.

Section 3

The Road to Level 7

In the last section, we talked about the need for everyone at all levels of the company to know what the organization's goals are. In our work with companies, we have found that it is common for the CEO or project leader to have a very good idea of what his or her goals are, but further down the chain of command within an organization, the employees have a very different idea.

A useful experiment that you can try in your own company is to ask your employees what they think the top priorities of the business are, right now. Let's say that you have identified your priorities as A, B, and C. Try a skip level review, going down yet another level of the company and surveying these employees about what the organization's most important goals are.

This diagram shows you a typical response that the manager who asks this question might get:

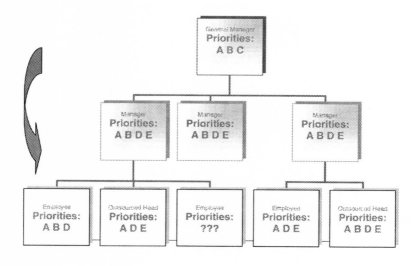

A review like this can be a real eye opener. A May 2005 Harvard Business Review article reported, "Individuals' work activities often do not reflect the current strategic priorities of the business leader ... and do not add to the bottom line."

"Ninety-five percent of the workforce does not understand the strategy."

Many CEOs have the right priorities, but the employees do not know what these priorities are—so the CEO does not reach his or her goals.

So for the purposes of example, let's say that your review turns out to be something like the diagram above, and that your well-intentioned employees are working hard, but they are not headed in the right strategic direction to deliver what the business needs.

Continuing the scenario above, now we'll assume that your company is at this moment dramatically behind where it should be when you compare target revenue to actual performance. Okay, so you put in what looks like a good project to drive revenue. The project delivers the revenue, but is three months behind schedule in achieving this goal. At the same time, several other very large orders have come in, and the company is now ahead of its revenue plan.

Your company is running ahead of revenue, so this is good news, right? Not exactly. As these new customers come on board, because your company has not built up the systems for this much growth, you will struggle mightily but be unable to deliver to this huge influx of demanding customers. Guess what happens? The customers become unhappy and march off to presumably happier hunting grounds elsewhere. You missed your target and you will be looking for a new job next year.

If your employees do not have a precise idea of what management's goals are, you will end up with a blurred strategic focus and results similar to the graph below:

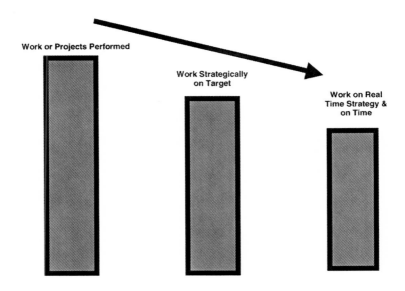

Just as you might have suspected, the amount of work that is done in alignment with your overall strategy and is performed on time is a small fraction of the total effort expended by your team. Why not change this and make your business the high performer that you know it can be? In Section 4, we will give you an understanding of the basics of a Level 7 performance management system—your ticket to high performance.

Section 4

Basics of a Successful Level 7 System

At this point, you are probably wondering exactly what a successful Level 7 system is, and how it can transform your business. Here is a definition:

A Level 7 system is an integrated, real-time, visual performance management system that strengthens management control of business priorities and projects and management's ability to execute activities to reach these priorities.

In contrast to the discouraging view that we showed you in Section 3, the diagram below shows you how a successful system helps the business aim at its strategic targets and deliver on time to achieve success:

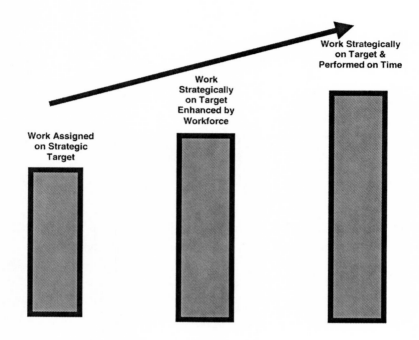

So, how do you bring these results to your business?

To start with, you as the business owner or project leader must think carefully about what it is you are trying to accomplish, and what will get you there.

The first step that we recommend is a "3 + 2 Analysis" in which you identify 1) your business' three key priorities—what it is that needs to happen for you to bring home the prize, 2) the number one challenge that is keeping you from getting where you want to be, and 3) the number one game-changing, long-term opportunity.

These three priorities, the one challenge, and the one opportunity will fit within some categories that are common to all enterprises, which we call Universal Key Business Measures, or KBMs.

For each business, five of these KBMs will be in specific areas: revenue, income, employees, customers, and compliance.

In addition to the universal measures, L7 systems leave space for you to select one or two customized areas that are unique to your company—the areas that drive key results in your business or with a specific project. For the Level 7 Performance Management System, we call these X-factors. In most business, the X-factors are the areas that provide your "secret sauce" and competitive advantage for your business or a project.

The five KBMs and the two X-factors will give you a total of seven priorities.

Keeping seven or less KBMs on the front burner at any one time will allow you to stay focused and effective, and to reach your objectives.

Each of the universal KBMs will be more fully explained later on in this book.

When you are establishing your Level 7 system, you will determine what the X-factors are for your organization.

After you complete the 3+2 Analysis and identify your company's X-factors, the next steps are to establish an owner for each KBM, either within your organization or using an outsourced provider, and to develop a concise business plan, which involves very specific goal setting in each area. Two pages or less for each goal is usually ideal. We provide a seven-step outline showing how this is done in the last section.

The goal, as always, is to simplify, to have the entire organization know what the priorities are, and to give everyone involved immediate feedback on how your organization is doing in terms of reaching your priorities.

Having one or two owners for each KBM and key project gives you as the CEO or manager the accountability—and each employee will be able to see exactly how he or she is doing on a daily basis. You can quickly or easily motivate him or her to turn on the steam, streamline the focus, or deftly switch to an area needing more attention.

There is some fine-tuning involved—let us show you how. In our organization, we use a process called targeting, innovation, and control. This process is very simple, extremely powerful, and will be easily understood by everyone in the company.

Typically targeting, innovation and control tie into your seven KBMs. When you are targeting, you set a goal for each KBM. For example, in the area of revenue, you might establish an annual goal in terms of dollars. In the area of customers, you might use a measure that looks at how closely your customer surveys track your expected results. There is amazing power in setting the numbers and letting the entire company know what they are, and this goes for every one of the goals that you set for each KBM.

This same process also works to deliver project execution excellence. Some companies use the system solely to drive their large project results. To drive project excellence, the KBM areas are the same.

During the innovation process, you pick the vital few focused projects and initiatives to get the results that you want. Focused projects drive ownership and speed of execution. This process can take some noodle time, but it is worth it—because in all likelihood, your competitors will not take the time to do it.

We recommend that you start with the projects that will have the greatest impact for you in the short term so that you can get some early momentum going, and also so that you have the greatest amount of time possible to get where you want to go.

Each project is assigned to a KBM. Sometimes, there is overlap, as a project may affect more than one area. When this happens, we suggest that you place the project in the area that has the highest potential impact and the highest priority for you.

When you have selected your projects and areas of highest impact, an ideal Level 7 system allows you to weigh each project based on its relative importance to your goals. This weighting continues as the system goes forward—and your progress toward your goals is measured against the weighting that you yourself select.

The control part of the process ties your targets to your projects in real-time. A top-notch system will allow you to know at all times where you are relative to all your KBMs, what the organization's top projects are, and the current status of these projects. It will then correlate all the measures and projects by weight.

This diagram gives you a view of how the steps that we have described above fit within the target, innovate and control process:

TARGET	INNOVATE	CONTROL

1) 7 Step Performance Plan (Part 1) Needs Analysis: Top three priorities/ challenge/ opportunity.

2) 7 Step Performance Plan (Part 2) Baseline and Measurement: Diagnosis of 3 top priorities relative to the 7 Key Business Measures (KBMs): Revenue, Compliance, Income, Customer, Employee, Two X-factors.

3) Build your performance web-based system with the 7 areas: Integrated to target, innovate and control results focused on top priorities and projects with owners.

4) Initiatives & Focused Projects: Prioritize improvements in top priority areas. Input weights and timing to track key initiatives and projects.

5) Ongoing System Operational: Now the company has a simple common process and visibility. Monthly one hour senior management meeting focused on the top three priorities, challenge and game changer opportunity...360° Performance Calls are also recommended.

You can build a performance management system yourself, or buy a system already built for you. The system should be Internet-based and have an internal database, and should correlate all your KBMs and projects instantly and visually. If you decide to build your web-based system from scratch, make sure all its elements—this means all the business measures and projects—are connected. The system should be normalized, meaning a standard scoring and weighting system is used. The system should have a history feature so you never lose a key project and always know what the targets, results, and owners were on any given day.

A proven system like this is commercially available; refer to www.L7pm.com for more information.

We have gone over a lot of information here. Below, we'll show you how the targeting process works in relation to your KBMs:

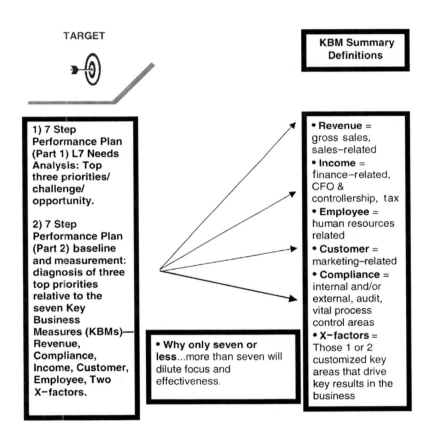

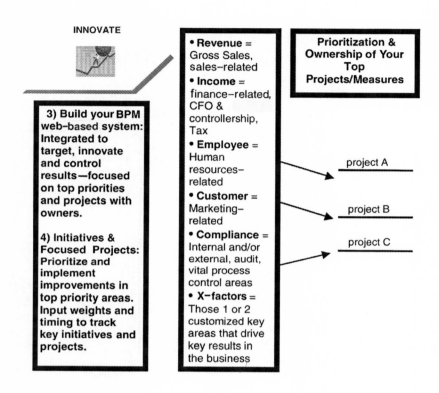

An important element of a Level 7 system is the ability to see what is happening with all your projects, and the progress towards your goals, at one time. Below, we show you an example of this—a Performance 360° View, which is what we use in our system.

Performance 360° View

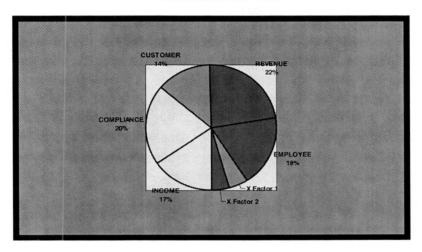

The Performance 360° view shows you exactly where you are in terms of your goals at any given time. The system works on a simple red, yellow, and green concept: when you see green (shown as gray in the chart above), this means that you are on target with your goals in that area. Yellow (white above) means that it's time to figure out what you need to do differently, because your approach is falling short of where you'd like to be. Red (black above) means that your business has fallen far behind in the path that you have set out for yourself, and it is time to take action immediately. The mechanics behind this graphic are explained in the technical section of this book, starting on page 69.

Data relevance and accountability are two key elements of any successful Level 7 system. As you will see in later chapters, KBM data should focus on the most important measurable data at that time for the company relative to the seven universal areas. This holds true if you are using the system for one major project, or to integrate the entire business. The frequency of updating can be anywhere from daily to annually, depending on data availability and relevance. The owner should input the key data to target elements. Key project data input should be done by the project owners who will provide information on percentage of project completion relative to the target milestones. Once people are trained on these basics, the open system can successfully grow organically. The most important factor here is that the key data elements are input by the owner who is closest to the data. This is counter-intuitive relative to much of today's performance management thinking. It will only take minutes for the owner to input the most important final data points, but when inputs are done by the real owner, you have real accountability. If you just use systems feeds, no one is really accountable; it is always a system error if there is a problem.

As a part of any Level 7 system, we recommend a meeting to diagnose the cause if a KBM "goes red." We call this a "root cause meeting." The purpose is to find the problem and develop a plan for the team to get refocused on priorities—so that you, the owner or manager can attain your goals. Addressing the problem sooner rather than later will assure that resources are deployed where they can do the most good, and will keep a small problem from developing into a nightmare that will consume resources and drain the ability to achieve in other areas.

With an at-a-glance view that is connected to all the KBMs and therefore all the company's important projects and initiatives, the manager and the employees can see very quickly where efforts need to be focused, and which projects are behind schedule or off track.

With the Performance 360° View, you get instant clarity of status, focus on what matters, and a roll-up and synthesis of all major measures.

In the figure below, you see the progression of an actual company's Performance 360° View over a three month period. By changing the business focus (depicted by the size of the slice and corresponding

KBMs and supporting projects), this organization was able to quickly impact results. You can see that as of November, which is in the green, the team has been able to stay on track to sustain the positive results that we start to see from September (mostly red) to October (mostly yellow).

Sample Performance 360° View Charts

September   October   November

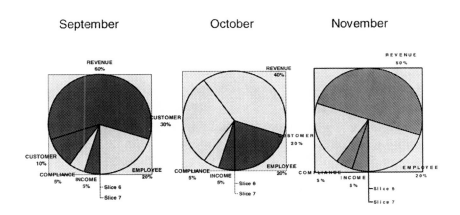

Implementing a Level 7 system means that the CEO and employees will sometimes be looking at a discouraging view of where things stand. The leader's willingness to get real and to be transparent with the employees about the business's weaknesses, with speed, is the key to the business being best in class in the long term. This ability we call *line of sight to the seven*. Moreover, the Performance 360° View solves a significant communication gap that exists in many companies between CEOs, project managers and employees.

In order to effectively use the system and the feedback that it gives to generate results, we recommend a system of what we call 360° business reviews. These are monthly meetings that usually involve the CEO and the senior management team and in general, they run for one hour. If the system is being used for a major project, these reviews would be with the project leader and the employee and vendor teams.

Each review starts with an overview of the three top priorities and the major challenge and opportunity. The group then takes a look at the current status of these initiatives and identifies whether or not the organization is green, yellow or red in the seven areas.

When we conduct these meetings with CEOs and managers, there is almost always a major "aha moment." What you as a manager look for is project distribution and status around your top priority areas. This is the real-time merger of strategy and tactics, or where the rubber meets the road, if you will. This is where the CEO or project leaders steer the ship in terms of priority percentage changes and major project distribution. As we have mentioned, in some cases the CEO may need to put a project on hold in one area to reallocate resources in another top priority area to right the ship.

Another important feature of any Level 7 system is the project tracking system. Here we show you one example of how this could be created for your organization.

Setting up Projects for Performance Excellence...

Performance Project Tracker

Project/Initiative Name: _____

Project/Initiative Owner: _____

Milestones/Tasks   Start Date   Finish Date/Actual Finish Date
1)_____
2)_____
3)_____
4)_____
5)_____
6)_____
7)_____

This technique is simple but very effective. You must make sure to select high impact projects and initiatives to drive your seven most important business areas. If you choose too many projects, you will lose focus. The rule of seven works here also. We have provided a template for your use at www.L7pm.com.

You will note in the example above that these projects all fall under the ownership of one person. It is important to have project managers, key milestones, and target start and finish dates for every initiative that you undertake.

Now you have a basic overview of how a Level 7 system works. Next, we will take a look at each of the seven KBMs and give you some tools and suggestions on how to focus your efforts so that your business can achieve record-setting results in each of these critically important areas.

Section 5

Key Business Measures for Your Business

In the model Level 7 system, the Universal Key Business Measures are revenue, compliance, customers, income, employees and two X-factors. The Level 7 CEOs and managers will continually be aware of the status of progress towards their goals in each of the seven KBM areas. They will also know which of the key projects are the ones that are driving results.

Revenue

Let's take a look at the first KBM—revenue.

Revenue growth will need even more attention in the new world, with increasing competition coming from all sides.

Here is a little exercise to help you assess your current level, anywhere from Level 1 to Level 7, to see where you need to focus your efforts in this vitally important area.

In this and all the surveys that follow, a common rating system is used: 1 is very poor, 2 is poor, 3 is unsatisfactory, 4 is satisfactory, 5 is good, 6 is very good, and 7 is excellent.

Level 7 Revenue Needs Analysis Self-Assessment

	1	2	3	4	5	6	7

Target:

- How would you rate the business' current ability to surpass revenue expectations?

  1   2   3   4   5   6   7

- Business' current ability to know revenue and backlog results vs. plan, at any given time (real-time)?

  1   2   3   4   5   6   7

Innovate:

- Rate the business' ability to create, sustain and grow the best practices, initiatives and projects across and throughout the business:

  1   2   3   4   5   6   7

- Do revenue innovations and initiatives come from all employees?

  1   2   3   4   5   6   7

Control:

- Does the business have clear owners for your revenue initiatives and targets?

  1   2   3   4   5   6   7

- How would you rate the business' current quality and effectiveness of basic revenue process elements—i.e. sales planning rhythm, sales training and development, CRM/prospecting support, sales review performance, sales sourcing, sales process measures, SM development?

  1   2   3   4   5   6   7

Average Score: 1   2   3   4   5   6   7

Your response to the quiz will give you an idea of areas to pay attention to: the need to create a transparent process, the ability to develop projects from within your organization to reach your goals, your ability to refocus quickly if your initiatives are not working out, and the elements of your basic revenue process, such as how you run and manage your sales effort.

Here, we'll touch on just one critically important element fueling a successful revenue effort: it's a must that you develop a culture that encourages all employees to provide their ideas. Managers are surprised to learn that hidden strength can come from momentum that they did not know they had—specifically, we're talking about innovation from the quiet introverted people who may need to be invited to share the breakthrough ideas that they've developed.

As you make your business transparent to everyone and you are able to admit that at times things are not on target, you will build team spirit. This will consequently lift morale and drive action, thoughts, and innovation—which leads to the big mo, when you turn these ideas into plans.

Compliance

The second Level 7 KBM we will touch on is compliance, an area that has come to the forefront in the new world.

As with revenue, we'll start you with a self-assessment so that you can be thinking of what your status is in this key area.

Level 7 Compliance Needs Analysis Self-Assessment

				5	6	7

Target:

- How would you rate the business current vs. ideal compliance state?

  1   2   3   4   5   6   7

- Business' current ability to know compliance process results to plan, at any given time (real-time)?

  1   2   3   4   5   6   7

Innovate:

- Rate the business ability to create, sustain and grow the best practices/initiatives/projects across and throughout the business:

  1   2   3   4   5   6   7

- Do compliance innovations and initiatives come from all employees?

  1   2   3   4   5   6   7

Control:

- Does the business have clear owners for your compliance initiatives and targets?

  1   2   3   4   5   6   7

- How would you rate the business' current quality and effectiveness of basic compliance process elements—i.e. internal process controls, financial planning rhythm, (SOX if public), OSHA, security, equal opportunity, complying with antitrust?

  1   2   3   4   5   6   7

Average Score:

  1   2   3   4   5   6   7

The key to a successful compliance effort is prevention. How can you make this happen in your organization? As with improvements in the revenue area, clear visibility and transparency is the key. If your organization is mid-sized or large, or if your firm is small but you have higher than average compliance risks, we recommend that you put in place a compliance-focused ombudsperson or an ombuds-team to surface issues and to support your internal audit staff.

Compliance should encompass all activities and communications of a Level 7 CEO and company. Along with real-time measures, there should be support for compliance projects to improve control and increase compliance excellence. We also recommend a regularly scheduled compliance review rhythm.

Customers

Now let's turn to the third KBM, the focus of your business: your customer.

We'll begin with an instrument to help you look at where you are regarding your all-important customers.

Level 7 Customer Needs Analysis Self-Assessment

	1	2	3	4	5	6	7

Target:

- How would you rate the business' current ability to surpass customer expectations given current market challenges vs. your ideal state?

  1 2 3 4 5 6 7

- Business' current ability to know customer results to plan, at any given time (real-time):

  1 2 3 4 5 6 7

Innovate:

- Rate the business' ability to create, sustain and grow the best practice/ initiatives/projects across and throughout the business:

  1 2 3 4 5 6 7

- Do customer innovations and initiatives come from all employees?

  1 2 3 4 5 6 7

Control:

- Does the business have clear owners for your customer initiatives and targets?

  1 2 3 4 5 6 7

- How would you rate the business' current quality and effectiveness of basic customer process elements, i.e. customer plans, survey process, customer response system, new product and existing product development process, marketing CRM?

  1 2 3 4 5 6 7

Average Score:

  1 2 3 4 5 6 7

The most important thing we can tell you about providing service to your customers: you need to have an ongoing plan in place to find out what your customers think, and to use the information gained to your advantage. Most businesses don't take the time to do this.

It's a best practice to survey your customers on a regular basis, keep them updated on what you're doing with the information that you collect, and distribute and really use the information for the improvement of your product or service.

Income

The fourth KBM is income. As with the others, we'll start with a quiz.

Level 7 Income Needs Analysis Self-Assessment

1	2	3	4	5	6	7

Target:
- How would you rate the business' current ability to surpass income expectations vs. your ideal state?   1 2 3 4 5 6 7
- Business' current ability to know income results vs. plan at any given time (real-time):   1 2 3 4 5 6 7

Innovate:
- Rate the business' ability to create, sustain and grow new income best practice/ initiatives/projects across and throughout the business: 1 2 3 4 5 6 7
- Do income innovations and initiatives come from all employees?   1 2 3 4 5 6 7

Control:
- Does the business have clear owners for income initiatives and targets?   1 2 3 4 5 6 7
- How would your rate the business' current quality and effectiveness of basic income process i.e. financial plan and rhythm, expense budgeting, expense controls and systems, procurement, outsourcing?   1 2 3 4 5 6 7

- **Average Score:**   1 2 3 4 5 6 7

The key to meeting your targets in the income area is keeping your eye on the whole picture and continually adjusting your actions to reach your goals. If things are not going well on the income side of things, you need to closely monitor expenses and do what you can to build your reserves before a small problem becomes a large one.

Accountability and clear ownership is central to income maximization. Everyone must know what measures, projects and tasks they own.

We also recommend that the final income targets and key measures be input into your system by the CFO or Vice President of Finance directly. This guarantees that the CFO has a final look at all the critical numbers that he or she needs to own in order for the business to be successful.

Employees

The fifth KBM, employees, is an area that we will explore below with this self-test.

Level 7 Employee Needs Analysis Self-Assessment

	1	2	3	4	5	6	7

Target:

- How would you rate the business' current ability to surpass employee goals and expectations given current status vs. your ideal state?

  1   2   3   4   5   6   7

- Business' current ability to know employee results to plan, at any given time (real-time):

  1   2   3   4   5   6   7

Innovate:

- Rate the business' ability to create, sustain and grow the best practices/initiatives/projects across and throughout the business:

  1   2   3   4   5   6   7

- Do employee innovations and initiatives come from all employees?

  1   2   3   4   5   6   7

Control:

- Does the business have clear owners for your employee initiatives and targets?

  1   2   3   4   5   6   7

- How would you rate the business' quality and effectiveness of basic employee process elements, i.e. employee human resource review, recruitment, performance measurement, performance reward and recognition, communications, 360° reviews, community involvement plan?

  1   2   3   4   5   6   7

Average Score:

  1   2   3   4   5   6   7

We use the term employee instead of "human resources" because our goal is to break down the perceived silos between departments. Matters relating to employees, as well as the other KBM areas, should be considered and owned by every employee within the organization. Getting people into "one bucket thinking" about the overall health of the business is a key to success in the new decentralized business world. That is why educating everyone on the seven universal KBMs is critical.

There are several keys to a Level 7 effort on the employee front, including encouraging innovation from every employee every day, creating both individual and collective accountability simultaneously, and creating a true merit-based reward system. Force yourself to resist the natural tendency to build a bureaucracy. Reward individuals for driving your KBM results. This creates an open system and meritocracy, which is very powerful. Team activities and compensation tied to your KBMs will give every employee the ownership and belief that his or her contribution matters—and this, of course, will lead to improved results.

In addition, a Level 7 company will regularly survey its employees and customers. The key to success here is acting on the results with real changes in how you do things, and bringing the information learned and the plan for how you will apply the new knowledge into all your employee communications. A survey without follow-up and information sharing is a waste of your time, and is a missed opportunity to share your message with those who need to see it the most—your employees.

The last two KBM areas are the X-factors. Ironically, many companies never figure out what the measures are that make them the most unique or those that would truly drive their business. But with your newfound knowledge, of course you will not make this mistake!

In order to use the self-assessment below, you will need to first establish what the X-factors are for your business. As a refresher: the X-factors are the two key long or short term areas that make your company unique.

These are the KBM measures that drive and focus your true competitive advantage or save you from decline. For a software company, an X-factor may be software development. For another company it may be operations. If you are using the system for one major project, the X-factor of the project would be the two top priority areas of the project that you want to measure.

Once you have your X-factors established, answer the questions below to see where you stand currently.

Level 7 X-factor Needs Analysis Self-Assessment

	2	3	4	5	6	7

Target:
- How would you rate the business' current ability to surpass X-factor targets?

1 2 3 4 5 6 7

- Business' current ability to know what the X-factors are & results to plan, at any given time (real-time):

1 2 3 4 5 6 7

Innovate:
- Rate the business' ability to create, sustain and grow the best practices/ initiatives/projects across and throughout the business:

1 2 3 4 5 6 7

- Do X-factor innovations and initiatives come from all employees?

1 2 3 4 5 6 7

Control:
- Does the business have clear owners for your X-factor initiatives and targets?

1 2 3 4 5 6 7

- How would you rate the business' current quality and effectiveness of basic X-factor process?

1 2 3 4 5 6 7

1 2 3 4 5 6 7

Average Score:

Level 7 CEOs and managers simultaneously know the status of all seven areas and the key projects that drive them.

With a Level 7 system, you have the agility of a small company and the power of a large one. When you achieve Level 7, you truly merge strategy and tactical execution—every day—for top results.

Section 6

Reaching Level 7—Putting it All Together

This section will help you put all seven levels and skills together to help your business reach Level 7.

The last step, although it sounds counterintuitive, is to go to the beginning and see if you are headed where you want to go. We started with the 3 + 2 Analysis—identification of the core top three priorities and the top challenge and long-term opportunity for your business or project. We have looked at the core KBMs. We have talked about the projects related to them. In a healthy business, these projects, challenges and opportunities continually change. Now, we ask you to integrate them with the parts of your business that seldom change: your business' identity, vision and slogan.

Each of these qualities is best defined in one sentence.

Internal identity, as we define it, captures the unique core competencies of your business. Quality, speed, price, and differentiation are the factors that comprise identity. Examples of companies that excel in these four dimensions are found in the retail world.

At Nordstrom's, you know you will always find quality merchandise.

At McDonalds, you know you are going to get served quickly, with speed.

A good example of a company that focuses its identity in price is Wal-Mart—when you walk in you know you are getting a good buy.

At Sharper Image, the focus is on differentiation—unique, differentiated products that are useful to the consumer.

Conversely, think of Montgomery Ward, if you can remember back that far. The merchandise that it sold was not the lowest price *or* the highest quality. The company was not about speed, and what it sold was not unique. Montgomery Ward tried to be all things to all people, and no surprise—the company faltered.

You need to pick your core dominant identity, taking into account each of the four factors of quality, speed, price and differentiation. Some companies try to differentiate a little bit in each of these areas, and never decide on a core identity. Unless they have a monopoly, usually these companies ultimately fail.

We define the slogan as a sentence that describes your business to your customer. The slogan describes the company's focus and customer-facing messaging—"We deliver computers made your way globally on time, every time."

The future of a company is a description of the type of ideal company you are building. Here is an example of a future statement: "Within three year, Terico Corporation will be a $600 million dollar revenue company, the leading national manufacturer of healthcare products to hospitals in the world."

Below is the seven-step plan to help you pull it all together in your quest to become a Level 7 business. You can see that Steps 4-7 fit well with all the work you have done thus far.

The 7 Step Performance Plan

Target-Your Business Core Identity

Definition: Select your #1 and #2 core identity

Example: Nature Quest is a customer-focused company with unsurpassed quality.

4 Areas: Quality, Speed, Price, or Differentiation

Target-Your Business Ideal Future & Core Values

Definition: A sentence on the ideal business you are building

Example: Within two years, Connecticut Home Corp. will be an $80 million national home services company specializing in manufacturing and distributing unique home products to baby-boomers.

Notes: Growth plans ($), market and product vision

(Attach core values statement if applicable)

Target-Your Business Slogan

Definition: A sentence that describes your business to your customers (i.e. your slogan)

Example: Home Products for Life

Notes: describes the company's focus and customer-facing slogan

<table>
<tr><td></td><td>Target-Your Key
Business Measures
(KBMs)</td></tr>
</table>

•*Compliance:*	*Compliance Survey Score to Target of 6*	*6.2/6.0*	*Semi-Annual*
•*Customer:*	*Customer Survey Score to Target of 5*	*5.1/5.0*	*Quarterly*
•*Employee:*	*Employee Survey Score to Target of 5*	*5.5/5.0*	*Quarterly*
•*Income:*	*Income to Target of 100% of Monthly Budget*	*92%/100%*	*Monthly*
•*Revenue*	*Revenue to Actual Monthly $ Target*	*$32MM/$28MM*	*Monthly*
•*X1:*	*Profit Per Employee to Target of $1MM*	*$.8MM/35*	*Monthly*
•*X2:*	*New Products per Quarter to Target of 1*	*.8/1*	*Monthly*

Notes: Numeric with target to actual … with a time frame

Innovate-Your Business
Ideas to Drive Your Key
Measures

•*Compliance:* *Start to survey all employees in January and all C level executives have individual plans*

•*Customer:* *Start cross referral program with both major product lines, expand into UK in Q2*

•*Employee:* *Hire Compliance Leader Q1, hire UK GM Q2, execute on 3 major survey findings*

•*Income:* *Cut cost in product line 2 by 10% by Q2, outsource product line 3 in by Q4*

•*Revenue:* *Execute on Acquisition Big Apple, sales contest, campaign UK telemarketing*

•*X1:* *Hold headcount in South region*

•*X2:* *Product X2 completion in Q2*

Notes: Ideas that set the direction of the projects

Control-Your Key Business Projects

•*Compliance:*	*Project Compliance Survey*	*Completion date Q2*
•*Customer:*	*Project UK*	*Completion date Q1*
•*Employee:*	*Project Big 3 Employee Survey*	*Completion date Q3*
•*Income:*	*Project 10 Cut*	*Completion date Q1*
•*Revenue:*	*Project Big Apple*	*Completion date Q3*
•*X1:*	*Project SE Productivity*	*Completion date Q2*
•*X2:*	*Project X2*	*Completion date Q2*

Notes: Name of project, key tasks up to 7, with start and finish

Control-Your Monthly 360° Business Priorities

#1 Priority: Increase Revenue 5% in Q1

#2 Priority: Complete Project Big Apple

#3 Priority: Implement compliance survey

#1 Challenge: Revenue in product line 2

#1 Long Term Opportunity: Project Big Apple

The seven step performance plan template is available to download for your use at www.L7pm.com.

With a Level 7 performance plan and system in place working for you, your business is now in a position to operate and grow stronger and faster domestically and globally. Your new system will allow you to enjoy the power of decentralization while maintaining control and accountability.

CEOs must now create real time
control in a flat global world

To assist you in your journey to Level 7, in the back of the book we have provided you with prescriptions and resources. If you have started to implement the Level 7 solution principles, you have started to increase control of your priorities in your business. With a focused consistent effort, you and your company will soon be enjoying the benefits of Level 7 performance.

The seven step priority plan, your new performance management web-based system, and your 360° business reviews will give you a great start towards achieving Level 7. You're on your way!

Larry's Level 7 Story

To illustrate the concepts that we have explained throughout this book, here we share the story of Joe and Larry and their companies. In this allegory, Joe is a new world leader (e.g., a Level 7 leader) and Larry is a traditional manager. Larry's story is the norm and not the exception today. Both Joe and Larry will help you on your journey and show you the steps you need to take in order for your business reach Level 7.

Larry is the CEO of a company, ABC Doors, that he purchased 15 years ago. ABC manufactures, distributes and installs overhead doors for commercial, residential, and municipal facilities in forty states. After the initial phase of his ownership, Larry had many years of good results, but the company has not performed well for the last four years. Competition is coming from many directions. He has used up many of his personal reserves and is wondering if he "still has it." Larry has four children, ranging in ages from seven to nineteen. He had to utilize his 401K money and the college funds he had set aside for the kids to make his business payroll over the past year. The cash situation in the household is becoming more acute, and the family has started to cut back on its non-essential purchases. If the trends continue, Larry will need to look at liquidating his business.

Larry has tried to sell his business for the last two years with no serious takers. The stress in his business has started to affect his marriage with his wife of twenty years, Jennifer. Jennifer has been supportive but wonders when they can replenish the college funds and return to the standard of living they used to enjoy. Jennifer has been a full-time mother for the last nineteen years, but she has felt the need to take a job to bridge the gap on their increasing debt payments. Recently, she secured a job selling pharmaceuticals by reconnecting with friends from college. Her new job requires her to travel beyond her original expectations and she is spending more time away from the family than is comfortable for her. She is worried that the children are not getting the quality time that they need with her. Larry has also had to travel more than he likes, because he is going out to push sales wherever he can.

Larry loves his business, and in the past he's been proud of his company and the jobs that he has created for his employees and their families. He has felt that in his way, he has helped the economy and has provided a valuable service to his customers. He genuinely cares about his customers and is puzzled as to why his proven approach is no longer translating into more sales for his company.

The harder Larry tries these days, the more it seems that his results suffer. He has tried downsizing, reorganizing, pitching new products, and personally doing the jobs he used to delegate.

In his desperation, Larry has begun searching for any kind of answer to save his business. He heard about Joe and his successful financial product company, Avalon Financial, from Bill, a friend from the neighborhood. Bill volunteered to call Joe and explain Larry's situation. When he did so, Joe readily agreed to meet with Larry.

Larry arrived at Avalon's sprawling headquarters and was immediately impressed with the clean and organized look of the business. The administrator, April, greeted him with a big smile, introduced herself and mentioned that she was also the office manager. April stated that Joe was having a "Coffee with Joe," an informal breakfast that he had with all new employees, but that he should be available shortly. Larry was immediately impressed with April's friendly and non-stressful demeanor and style. They chatted about the recent holiday. Since Larry wondered if the non-stressful atmosphere in the office meant that business was slow, he asked April how things were going.

April reported that Avalon was having a solid year and that revenue and operating profit were on track for the year. Revenue and customer measures were off the second quarter, she said, but with an increased focus in the third quarter, Avalon is now once again on plan or "green," as she put it.

She went on to say that "all of the our key measures are now back on track—the third quarter has some large targets, but we are in good shape to reach all seven of our key targets this year which is great, because I already have that holiday bonus spent in my mind!"

April glanced at her screen for a moment and then looked up and smiled. Larry had never heard of an office manager who had so much insight into the business or frankly seemed to care as much as she did. She spoke about Avalon and its goals as if it were her business, with a tone of pride in her voice. Larry was particularly impressed when she referred to the business' goals as "our targets."

April said Joe was ready to see Larry, so he followed her to Joe's office. Joe was looking out the window when Larry arrived and looked up and said with a smile, "It is a pleasure to meet you, Larry. Bill tells me you have four kids."

Larry asked about Joe's family, and Joe talked briefly about one of his children, a boy who has disabilities. Joe said that working out ways to help the son had brought he and his wife closer together. Larry and Joe spoke about their families and activities in the community for several minutes, and then Larry asked what Joe knew about ABC's situation. Joe reported that Bill had given him a quick summary, and he asked for more information.

Larry felt very comfortable quickly with Joe and gave him an overview of the gory details of his struggles with his business. After Larry finished, Joe asked him if he wanted to learn more about Avalon's secret weapon—the Level 7 system—in detail, or would he like a quick 30,000 feet overview. Larry said he wanted to take the big dive and learn about whether or not this system would apply to his business.

Joe explained that the best way to help Larry learn would be to set up meetings with what he called his KBM staff. Each of these people, he said, was jointly and separately critical to making the Level 7 system work, as were all his employees. The members of his team were Sam, Revenue Champion, Burt, Net Income Champion, Hayward, Compliance Champion, Gail, Employee Champion, John, Customer Champion, and Shulo, X-factor Champion. This new arrangement, Joe stated, had allowed Avalon to integrate operations and break down the old silos and buckets of functions and departments. He went on to say that getting everyone to feel part of the community was critical to Avalon's success. Avalon had spent significant time training all employees about the key elements of business, no matter which department their primary responsibilities were in.

Joe said that the job of each designated champion was to design the two-page plan for his or her area and to lead the business in the direction of staying "on plan" in their specific area. He further said that if the champions had to change the plan for unforeseen circumstances, they would be the people to lead the change.

Joe explained that five of the seven KBMs are the same for each business that has a Level 7 system—income, revenue, compliance, employees, and customers. The X-factors are customized for each business. The same principles also work for major projects.

Joe went on to explain that "one of the keys to success is knowing the phase your business is in." He went on to talk about the basics of his definitions of business phases. The seven phases are 1) Start-up, 2) Standardization,

3) Delegation, 4) Coordination, 5) Collaboration, 6) Sub-divisional phase, and 7) the Decentralized Community Phase. The Level 7 system works within any of the seven phases, Joe said, but "you must apply it differently depending on the phase. Basically the success of the earlier phase will cause problems at the end of the phase if you do not adjust within that time-frame."

Joe reported, "The second key to success is being a Level 7 leader and driving Level 7 throughout the business. Level 7 leaders know the status of their measures of success and the key projects driving these measures of success at all times. You can move mountains if you and your employees are focused on the same goals. These days, everything is changing so fast that you need a system that gives you information in real-time and correlates it simply for educated decision making with speed."

"The old strategic plan that sat on the shelf does not work in today's world. Strategy and tactics must merge and become real-time—this is what the Level 7 system will do for you. It is a time for a different strategy to effectively compete in this decentralized open world."

Larry asked a question about how the organization's priorities were determined. Joe responded, "The KBM areas for our company—income, revenue, compliance, employees, and customers—will always stay the same and our X-factors—profit-per-employee and new product development—rarely change, but I decide on a day-to-day basis what to emphasize that day. I am looking at the results constantly. Some days, I can see at a glance that our performance is dropping in one of these areas. This information is shared with all employees and we adjust our priorities accordingly. This is one of the most amazing features of the Level 7 system—I have the information I need at my fingertips to make decisions and to fine-tune our approach."

Larry felt a glimmer of hope. He was ready to learn about putting the Level 7 system in place at ABC. Could there really be hope for his beleaguered business after all?

Joe set up an appointment for Larry with Sam, Avalon's Revenue Champion. Joe said that before Larry could put a system in place at ABC that he needed to determine the current phase of his business and that Sam could help him with the "Grow Revenue Equation" for his business.

Larry arrived for his appointment with Sam. After they chatted, Larry asked Sam how the business was going. Sam replied, "We are having a strong year, and revenue and operating profit are on track for the year. Revenue and customer measures were off in Q2, which is something I paid a lot of attention to as the Revenue Champion, but with the help of the entire business focusing and pitching in with extra work, creativity and solutions, we were able to get back on track. My sales reps got leads from employees all over the company that turned into several closed deals. One of our operations managers helped us close a very large sale with a new operations support idea that we have now commercialized into the business as an additional service offering. We are now once again on plan, or green as we call it. All key measures are now back on track. Q3 has some large goals, but we are in good shape to get to our targets."

Larry was impressed with the amazing alignment of knowledge and focus from April, Joe and now Sam. They clearly were on the same page.

Sam asked Larry, "Are you ready to determine what phase your business is in?" When Larry replied in the affirmative, Sam explained that the KBMs of income, revenue, compliance, customer, employee and X-factor apply to all phases, but that the CEO or manager needs to know the phase the business is currently in to navigate the ship within the phase. Sam pulled out a chart of the seven phases that Avalon used.

Sam explained that the practices and the organizational design inverts with each phase, and this is where many managers start to lose revenue and productivity. They apply the practices and organizational design that made them successful in the last phase to the next phase, which usually produces inverted income. This is a more pleasant way of saying what is really going on—losses.

Sam asked Larry a series of questions. After analyzing Larry's existing business and products, they came to the conclusion that ABC was in Phase 2 but in danger of declining quickly to Phase 1 if changes were not made.

Larry talked about when the trouble had started. "Revenue and profits were growing fast. We had built an excellent way of providing service, and as the business got bigger, we tried to keep our original successful strategies and just do more. Our approach was very centralized, with standards and processes; everyone knew what to do and when to get my approvals. We grew a lot during this period. The success of the additional business was the major cause of the problems that started our decline. Since I made most of the major decisions, I started to have trouble keeping up. Then I lost two of my top managers. Then we lost a development company and a state contract—our second and third largest customers. When I exit-interviewed the managers who left, they said they loved the company, but had wanted more responsibility and needed more autonomy to lead, not the hand-holding situation that I had set up. I didn't think much of this at the time, because it seemed as though this had to do with them and where they were in their careers and not with our company, which at that time was doing exceptionally well."

Sam commented that he could see that when Larry had bought the company, it had very little leadership and process. His leadership and improved methods had turned it around. He further stated that it appeared that as the business had grown and moved into Phase 3 that the solutions of Phase 2 had caused the downturn in Phase 3. By the end of the day Larry for the first time had realized his own actions, not external factors, were the major factor in his company's downturn.

This was a real "aha moment" for Larry. He summed it up by saying:

"In my mind I had been blaming the economy, the employees, the customers, and even my wife on occasion, when in reality, I had made decisions that had a major impact on our downturn. I did not know the phase I was in, and I did not have a good handle on our measures of success and our key project status."

After a few hours of denial, Larry had reached an acceptance of the major causes of his problems. He had perhaps always known but forgotten somewhere along the way that most of the time, the leaders are the ones who can keep things growing and the business on track. It is often the leaders who can send the business downhill, or to the top of the mountain. If you can build leaders throughout the employee base, they can help right the ship as you go. Before you can do this you have to work through the phases.

Larry had learned that the speed of market growth and the economy would determine how quickly the leader must navigate through the phase changes. If there are declines in a market, product or niche, it is the leader's responsibility to determine if the decline is chronic or temporary. If it is chronic, the leader must reposition the business with new products, venture into new markets if possible, or in the worst case, shut the product line down.

Sam further questioned Larry about market information. Larry felt that the door market was still growing at a strong pace, with housing starts being projected to increase over the coming year. Several distribution facilities that could be potentially large customers were being developed in an area 50 miles from one of Larry's locations. Fortunately, despite his prob-

lems, Larry still had a solid competitive advantage, given his company's long history of excellent service and the range of products that ABC provided to different sectors.

Larry was so relieved to finally feel hope instead of the desperation and the sinking feeling that had been following him for the last few months. He asked Sam to help him do exactly what he needed to set up a Level 7 system for his business.

Sam began by giving some detail on the role of the KBMs in the Level 7 process. "All of the seven KBMs have the same look and feel. They are all correlated so we all get an instant read on the company's health. The overview also tells us what areas need attention. Here is a typical revenue dashboard for you to look at. My area was behind plan so it was red. Within 15% of plan is yellow and on or above plan is green. I was still confident that with everyone's help, I could make my original plan so I did not create a new one. The system stores the plans. This way we all have a reference point to measure our historical performance in relationship to our plan. If there is unforeseen change in the market or you really do not think you can make your original plan, it is okay to make a new one. If I am consistently setting lower target plans, something has gone wrong in that particular area and we need to take drastic action to correct it."

Sam further explained:

"The KBM and the system have a major review meeting rhythm. We call this the 360° Performance Review."

"We invite all the Champions, board members, and all key stakeholders to the meetings when possible. The system is always updated at fiscal close but is also updated whenever we have new numbers and inputs, and have project progress to update. The Champions, project and KBM owners all

make input. All inputs are tracked, giving everyone ownership in the system."

"Before we had the Level 7 system, the review meetings used to be annual, but now, we've realized that to keep up with the speed of change, we need to meet monthly. The meetings are short with almost no prep time required because the system has the full picture. We always highlight someone who executed on his or her targets well. If a KBM goes red, we also have a meeting ASAP to figure out why and adjust things accordingly. We call these "root cause meetings." It is OK to go red. But when you go red, you need to have a good idea of the potential root causes and to act on the challenge quickly. Before the 360° meetings, the CEO reweighs the KBMs and key projects so the whole business can get a focus on the top priorities. This tells everyone to pay attention and to apply resources where we need them to achieve success."

Larry reviewed the two-page seven-step performance plan in the area of income that Sam had prepared for Avalon. At this point, he realized that he had been so focused on immediate rescue for his company that he hadn't been comparing his results to his previous plans, and instead had been developing new plans willy-nilly every few weeks or even every few days to respond to crisis after crisis.

Larry went home to tell Jennifer all he had learned. When he got home he found a note from her on the kitchen counter: "Dear Lar, Great news! David called and said we are one of the top two finalists for the First Med bid we are working on. I am on my way to the airport and headed for Dallas, as John thinks we have a better chance of winning the account in person. Please pick the kids up ... they are over at Susie's. There is pot roast in the crockpot. I will call you late tonight when we get to Dallas. Love you, Jennifer." Larry had had last minute trips come up many times, but this was the first time he had experienced the situation from the other side. It was not a feeling that he particularly enjoyed.

In the next phase of his exploration of the Level 7 process, Larry went to see Hayward, Avalon's Compliance Champion. Hayward and Larry spoke for a few moments about their background. Larry found Hayward's background very interesting—he was a lawyer as well as a CPA. He had spent part of his career as a judge. After he moved back into the private sector, he had spend the last ten years in compliance. He was passionate about it.

Hayward began to talk about the field of compliance in general. He reiterated something Joe had told Larry, that:

"Compliance is the base of everything else that we do.... without the base, we have nothing."

Hayward asked Larry about ABC's current phase of business and what his key measures of success were, and his current compliance leadership and system. Larry replied that his CFO had the responsibility for compliance in addition to her other duties.

Hayward encouraged Larry to make compliance excellence one of his top seven measures of success. He reiterated that it would send a message to the entire company, and impact how each employee would conduct his or her business on a daily basis.

Hayward talked about how Level 7 is built on transparency. It creates a line of sight and a closed loop process to prevent issues.

He also recommended Larry set up a system of anonymous feedback to surface issues early, as well as an all-employee survey on compliance.

Hmm, much more to think about. Larry's next visit at Avalon sent him to see John, the Customer Champion. John, as had the others, invested time up front to get to know Larry as a person. Before Larry asked, John gave him an update on the company and talked openly about the customer KBM being yellow and not green.

John reported, "We are having a good year—revenue and operating profit are on track for the year. Revenue and customer measures were off in Q2, but we were able to get them back on track in Q3. However, as of last week, in the beginning of Q4, they've gone yellow." John did not seem nervous about this, but almost excited about attacking the problem. He talked about the root cause of the problem being Avalon's fourth largest customer giving them a "three score" on their post-delivery survey. A quarterly survey of all major customers was an important part of Avalon's Level 7 strategy.

John had already called the disgruntled customer and had found out that one of Avalon's vendors had missed product delivery by a day, thus the under-budget score. Delving into the problem further, he found that the vendor had not only missed the project delivery date, but had failed to let Avalon know that the product would arrive late. John was meeting with Joe to talk about a vendor change in that particular area.

Summing up where Avalon's position was at that moment, John stated: "Q4 has some large targets, but we are in good shape to achieve to our goals. We need to make sure our customer is satisfied with our fix on this problem."

Three days later, Larry met with Burt, Avalon's Income Champion. Burt was more of a "get right to it" personality. Larry picked up on this quickly and jumped right into the task at hand.

The first question Burt asked, like John, concerned Larry's current business phase. Larry shared that he was in Phase 2, but was quickly moving backward into Phase 1. He also talked to Burt about the phase analysis that Sam had worked on with him, and gave a quick history of his company and its current challenges.

Burt asked about Larry's expense control systems. He noted that in Phase 2, particularly in combination with declining trends, that expense control is of vital importance. Larry told Burt of his existing accounting and budgeting processes. Burt could tell right away that Larry had an expense "line of sight" problem. Larry's budget and approval process was not clearly defined.

Burt talked about the how the Level 7 system had resulted in dramatic improvements to Avalon's income.

Avalon was a private corporation, but the back-to-basics and transparency line of sight of the Level 7 system were big hits with its bankers and private investors. In fact, the bankers were so impressed that they had recommended the system to several other clients.

Burt talked in general terms about how many companies were realizing that excessive debt leverage payments are a value and long-term net income killer. He stated that the keys to success were going back to the basics of caring for customers, making money, controlling expenses at all phases responsibly and sharing this information in an easy-to-grasp way with all the employees. He noted that this was why all employees had been trained in all the seven KBM business basics, and in how to run projects. He added, "The difference today is that you need to correlate and synthesize information and feedback much faster—and that is what Level 7 does for us. Even in the early phases this is critical today. The goal is to get the business to Phase 7, but you need to work through all of the phases. The thing today is that some of the phase changes are in weeks, not years."

Burt added, "Using the Level 7 system is critical to maximizing performance in all phases, but how you apply it will change by the phase." With

Larry's business declining to Phase One, simplification and going back to core business products and expense controls would be key, Burt noted.

As Larry drove home, he felt like he was back in his first year of graduate school again. He also knew that Burt was right. When Larry got home, he told Jennifer what he had learned about Burt's "back-to-basics with Level 7 speed" lesson. Jennifer started to feel a little hopeful about ABC's future also. She and Larry decided to put their own home expense budget together, which was a first. That night they decided to take a swim together for the first time in years.

A few days later, Larry arrived at Avalon's sprawling headquarters to see Gail, the Employee Champion. She was very congenial and conversational. She knew Jennifer from a group at the school that both of their children attended, and asked several questions about how things were going.

After exchanging pleasantries, Larry asked Gail about current trends. Gail said almost the same things as the others, about revenue and customer measures being down in Q2, but back on track in Q3, and about the company being well-positioned to meet its targets in Q4, despite the ambitious goals.

Larry wondered if the employee measures would be as important to his employees as they were in a larger company like Avalon. Joe's company had over double the employees that ABC did. Gail told him that she had learned that training all employees on business basics and paying attention to employee issues is very important, and even more important for small to mid-sized companies because one or two key departures can bring down the ship. Ouch. This made total sense to Larry, as he just experienced this problem firsthand with the departure of two of his key people.

Gail also talked about how the employees liked the Level 7 system as it allowed them to see the bigger picture and how their work fit into that bigger picture. Now, everyone feels like they are a part of a community with common goals.

She said that the system helps to eliminate bureaucracy, and drives a meritocracy, as bonuses are tied to real performance based on the key measures of success and on how employees performed on their projects—projects that drive key business measures.

She said that employee morale survey scores were up significantly after implementing the Level 7 system. She said, "the employees all feel they are important, because they have all been trained on the seven key business areas and process. Now that we have taught them all the common business language and made the process easy for them, terrific projects and innovations are popping up all over the company. It has a feeling of community that people like. We have taught them all how to fish. They can use these skills for the rest of their life no matter where they are working."

As he continued to learn more, Larry was itching to get back to ABC and put the system in place, but he had one more visit to make to complete his research at Avalon.

Larry met Shulo, the X-factor Champion, early one morning for coffee in the conference room at Avalon. Shulo, as had the others, spent time getting to know Larry and his company before he launched into his KBM discussion and teachings.

Larry was wondering if today might be the day that he would see the Level 7 system break down, since two days before, John had shared that the customer area had gone yellow. He asked Shulo the million-dollar question about how things were going. Shulo gave the same answer about the previous year's results, but he added: "As of last week, our customer and our X-factor indicators have gone yellow."

Like John, Shulo did not seem anxious, but intrigued and ready to solve the problem. He already had the information about the root cause of the X-factor issue, and the fourth largest customer giving Avalon a three score on the post-delivery survey. He also knew why the customer was displeased. A meeting of the Champions team had taken place yesterday, and the group had developed two alternatives to solve the problem—one involved asking the customer if they wanted Avalon to replace the vendor, and the other, asking the customer whether they would prefer a computer lock on the promise times. Shulo felt confident that the targets could be met in the fourth quarter with this action plan in place.

It was time for Larry to synthesize his learning. Over several weeks, Larry's Level 7 management studies yielded three major findings. First, he came to the realization that blaming circumstances and his employees were only hurting ABC's progress. Much of what had happened was a result of strategy and projects that used to work in a different time and phase. Second, neither he nor his employees had clearly identified their top KBM measures and projects. He now understood the new breed of decentralized competitors that were capitalizing on the new technology and process integrations. Additionally on this point, Larry had no system to continually keep track of the status of his projects. Given this, there was minimal accountability or visibility down the line. Third, and most importantly, he was very excited about the realization that his situation and company were fixable. Ah, relief at last! Larry and Jennifer went out to dinner at their favorite restaurant to celebrate.

As a wrap-up, Larry met with Joe and thanked him. Joe said he would like to stay in touch as Larry progressed with his company. Larry was very impressed by Joe's generosity of his own time and that of his employees, and he asked him what he could do in return. Joe's only requests were for Larry to let people know about the quality of his company, and to send him a sales referral if he ran into someone who could use Avalon's services. Larry was more than happy to do both of these things. As he and Joe parted ways, they agreed to play golf in the upcoming summer.

It took some hard work to get everyone reoriented, but three months later, ABC Doors was fully trained and "Level seven-ized". Revenue was starting to pick up. Morale appeared to be coming back after years of decline. The KBM areas were solid. The employees knew the status of each KBM area and the key projects in each area. Seven months later, ABC had executed its first record quarter in years. Although he had thought it would never happen again, Larry was now enjoying the business.

The home front was also changing for the better. Jennifer, who had become intrigued with Larry's glowing reports about Level 7, started helping with the business and the management system. With the stress level down at home and a regular paycheck coming in, Larry, Jennifer, and the children were able to spend more time together.

Later, Jennifer started her own medical supply business using the Level 7 system. She and Larry became much more active in their church and community over time.

Over the next few years, business life for Larry and Jennifer of course had its challenges, but they were able to avoid most major problems before they happened. When a problem did occur, they could respond quickly with a solution. Both of their business flourished.

Larry and Jennifer experienced a moment that brought everything full circle years later when their youngest son Ethan, now a senior in college, asked them about the Level 7 management system. They responded as Joe had years before. "Do you want an overview or do you really want to learn the system?" Larry asked. Ethan replied that he really wanted to learn. Larry happily responded: "Let's get started."

R/x: Eighteen Prescriptions to Help Your Business Reach Level 7

R/x 1: Drive speed for growth in your seven most important priority areas by knowing if you are green, yellow, or red—and why.

R/x 2: Know the status of all of your top seven projects—the key projects that drive your seven KBM areas.

R/x 3: Get speed by scoping down projects and timelines, building Level 7 fundamentals to avoid crisis, and gaining momentum.

R/x 4: Keep outsourced partners on task and on time through a common set of priorities and visibility to the status of those priorities.

R/x 5: Face reality and let your people know when you are veering off plan in order to get all hands on deck to help reach your goals. Teach the entire employee base the business process fundamentals and how to run a project.

R/x 6: Get help if you need it. Hire or outsource an expert if you need one—don't be your own brain surgeon.

R/x 7: Encourage innovation from all employees and reward the people who create innovation that works.

R/x 8: Do not focus on more than seven measures at once—employees will not process and correlate more than seven continuous processes at once without losing focus.

R/x 9: To gain acceptance of the Level 7 system, involve all members of the team in setting up the system and key measures.

R/x 10: Bring the compliance message into all your employee communications.

R/x 11: Drive home the point that compliance is every employee's business.

R/x 12: Utilize the Level 7 principles and a system that makes an individual as well as the whole organization accountable for measures and projects.

R/x 13: Know what your customers think by asking them on a regular basis, and systematize the process of collecting this information and acting on the information.

R/x 14: Be aware of trends, so that you can make changes early on to improve your results.

R/x 15: Utilize outsourcing to drive your net income and productivity.

R/x 16: When starting with a Level 7 system, always start small, with the most important projects, and build out from the core.

R/x 17: Use the system for execution excellence of major projects and for total company performance.

R/x 18: The open system creates a community of employees who now can "fish for themselves" with a common language and measurement system. Let them innovate and fish. Let the community grow and take its shape. You will be amazed at the power of the open system, but still be able to maintain control through accountability.

Level 7 Performance Management System Nuts and Bolts

Here is an overview of the Level 7 Performance Management System, developed by L7 Performance Management. The L7 Performance Management System has been designed and is fully aligned with the Level 7 principles to help companies reach record results. This section takes a more technically detailed look at the Level 7 principles and systems. A special thanks to Lawrence Waugh for his excellent technical counsel and writings in this section. Here are selected excerpts from the L7PM training manual. The full manual, along with the system and information on finding or becoming an L7 Partner is available through the L7 web site at www.L7pm.com. One of the problems with some business books is that they lay out all the challenges and issues, but do not provide any real solutions. Below, we explain the nuts and bolts of a system that gives you the tools to thrive in this new decentralized business environment.

Overview

The L7 Performance Management System (L7PMS) is designed to allow easy visualization and implementation of the Level 7 management process. The system is set up to be used by managers, individual contributors, and all others involved with an organization. It allows contributors to organize, monitor, and control their work. L7PMS allows managers to quickly identify potential problem areas and monitor areas of importance. With the system, all other individuals in the organization will know what the key opportunities and initiatives are, and how the company is tracking toward its goals.

Structure

In general, the L7PMS creates a "tree," like a directory on a hard drive, which represents the major areas of your business or a major project broken down into increasing levels of granularity. Some categories may fall under two KBMs, and the system can easily accommodate this. It also allows for sub-categories, however, no category may have more than seven sub-categories for simplification. We recommend that you start with just a few key projects at first and then over time, increase the number of projects. The entire purpose of the L7PMS is to allow you to easily visualize, interact with, and manipulate this tree. There are several different aspects of this application, described below.

L7 Scoring

The L7PMS is based around the concept of the L7 score—a number from 1 to 7 (inclusive) that represents the health of key measures and projects of the company. In general, an L7 Score of 1 is very poor, 2 is poor, 3 is Unsatisfactory, 4 is Satisfactory, 5 is Good, 6 is Very Good, and 7 is Excellent. These ranges will often be displayed as red, yellow and green.

At the lowest level, "files" of the L7PMS tree are given L7 scores, either directly (by inputting a number) or indirectly, by having the L7 score automatically calculated based on progress on a project, or how well target metrics match actual ones.

As you progress through the tree, files are aggregated into "folders," and each folder derives its L7 score from the scores of its files, based on a weight that is assigned to each file. Likewise, folders are aggregated into other folders, and so on, through the tree, until you reach the "Root"—the "roll-up" of all of the initiatives and data points being tracked.

Essentially, beginning with the Root folder, each folder divides into 1-7 up to seven other folders, each of which is weighted appropriately. This subdivision continues through the tree until you reach a file, which represents either raw data (such as revenue), or project data. These files receive an L7 score, while percolates back through the tree until it reaches the Root which represents the health of the measures.

Level 7 Web Application

The L7PMS Web Application is accessed via Microsoft Internet Explorer or Firefox browsers.

Logging In

Upon accessing the L7PMS, the system will prompt you for a user name and password in the security screen. Entering your user name and password will bring you to the "Root" view, which will look something like this:

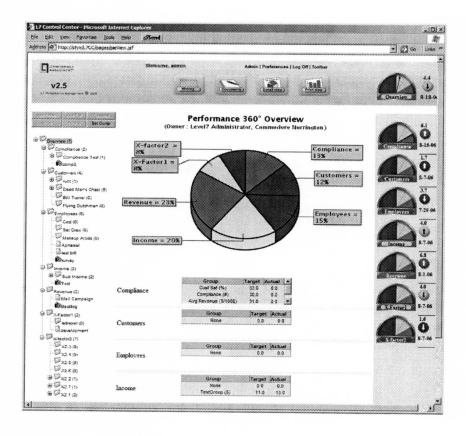

The various sections of this screen are divided into four sections, which are explained in detail below: the top bar (on top), the tree browser (on the left), the gauges (on the right), and the views (in the center). For now, just notice that the applications give several different ways to look at the performance of your business. Even without going through this guide, you can probably tell at a glance how the company in question is doing: "Fair"—but with a few areas of concern: notably "Employees" and "X-factor 1."

Views

There are four major views in the L7PMS. These are "360°," "Detail," "Project," and "Data." Project and Data views show the user the status of a project or data file, respectively. Folder and detail are two different ways of viewing a folder (i.e. a non-file). The Level 7 CEO knows at a glance the status of his or her key areas and projects.

Folder Views

Performance 360° View

The "standard" view is the Performance 360° View. This view provides a high-level view of the folder in question by showing it as a pie chart, with each slice representing a child folder or file. The color of the slice represents the status of that folder/file, and the size of the slice represents its relative weight. Beneath the pie chart, the relevant "groupings" for that folder will be shown. Groupings are discussed in the section on Data Files.

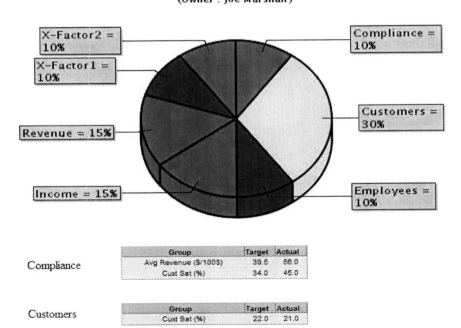

Performance 360° Overview
(Owner : Joe Marshall)

X-Factor2 = 10%

X-Factor1 = 10%

Revenue = 15%

Income = 15%

Compliance = 10%

Customers = 30%

Employees = 10%

Compliance	Group	Target	Actual
	Avg Revenue ($/100S)	39.5	56.0
	Cust Sat (%)	34.0	45.0

Customers	Group	Target	Actual
	Cust Sat (%)	22.0	21.0

Clicking any slice of the pie chart will "drill down" into that slice—showing you the status of that folder or file.

The 360° View is the default view, but if a user is viewing a Detail View, they can return to the 360° View by clicking the "360° View" tile in the top bar. Once in the 360° View, you will stay in that view until you click the "Detail View" tile.

Details View

The Details View represents another view of a Folder, with more data. In the example above, we can see that the "Employees" slice from the 360 view is red, so below, we have clicked on it, and then selected the "Details View." Below, you can see the three elements that make up the Employee folder.

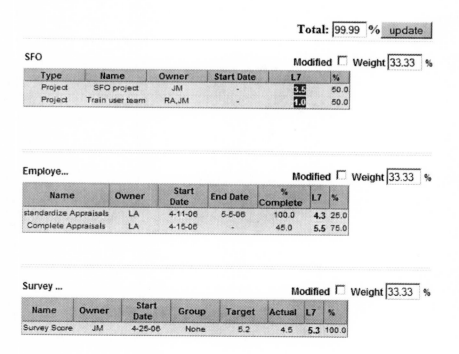

Total: 99.99 % update

SFO   Modified ☐ Weight 33.33 %

Type	Name	Owner	Start Date	L7	%
Project	SFO project	JM	-	3.5	50.0
Project	Train user team	RA,JM	-	1.0	50.0

Employe...   Modified ☐ Weight 33.33 %

Name	Owner	Start Date	End Date	% Complete	L7	%
standardize Appraisals	LA	4-11-06	5-5-06	100.0	4.3	25.0
Complete Appraisals	LA	4-15-06	-	45.0	5.5	75.0

Survey ...   Modified ☐ Weight 33.33 %

Name	Owner	Start Date	Group	Target	Actual	L7	%
Survey Score	JM	4-25-06	None	5.2	4.5	5.3	100.0

Note that there are three entries: the "SFO" folder, the Employee Appraisals project, and the Survey Score data file. (Projects and Data files are discussed below.) Each of these has a slightly different representation. You can tell what the type of each file by looking at the Tree Browser on the left.

The Folder view ("SFO" above) shows the elements under that folder: their types, names, owners' initials, a start date, the current L7 score (backgrounded with the appropriate color), and the relative weight of each project under the SFO folder (e.g., in this example, they both contribute equally).

The Employee Appraisal project file lists, for each task in the project, the name, owner(s) initials, target start date, target end date, current status (i.e. % complete), the current L7 score, and the relative weight of that task within the project. Note that "Complete Appraisals" contributes 75% of the weight, while "Standardize Appraisals" only contributes 25%. Therefore, the L7 score is more dependent on completing them than standardizing them.

The Survey Score data file shows the current target/actual values for the survey. The Survey Score data file actually has three target/actual values, but the other two are in the future. The L7PMS will show you the target/actual for the most recent period—that is, for the date that has most recently passed.

The Details View is entered from the 360° View by clicking on the "Detail View" tile in the top bar. Once you are in the Details View, you will stay there until you either visit a file folder (which has no Details View), or click the "360° View" tile.

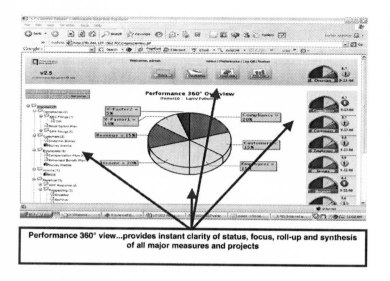

Performance 360° view...provides instant clarity of status, focus, roll-up and synthesis of all major measures and projects

This view gives you detail showing each KBM area and the projects that fall within that area. Even though overall, the compliance area at this company is on target, if we look at the information given in the detail view more closely, we can see that the SEC filings and EPA fillings projects are occurring on schedule, but that the stock option plan needs some attention.

You will also notice that on the right of this view that there are several indicators—one for each KBM—that we call dashboards. The dashboard at the very top gives you an overview of how your company is doing, right now, in relation to your goals. As you move down the chart, you can see that in this particular example, the business is doing well in the compliance and revenue areas but is in yellow territory for the customers, employees, and income KBMs.

Here we show you how the project file view gives you instant information on your progress toward your goals. If this were your system, you could click on any of the projects listed in the folders on the left-hand side and immediately gain information on how your company was progressing towards your goals in this area. In the example shown, the company is doing quite well in reaching its revenue targets. The only area that is behind is the RFP response, and since this is weighted only as a small portion of the overall effort, the company is in the green—in more ways than one—in this particular KBM.

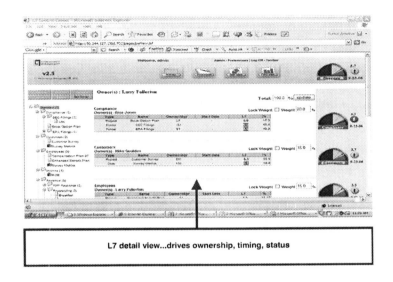

L7 detail view...drives ownership, timing, status

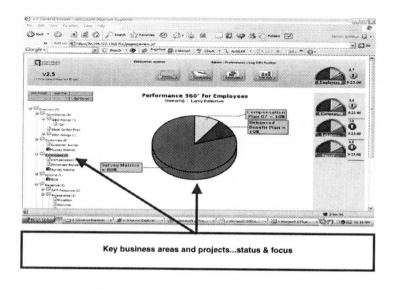

Key business areas and projects...status & focus

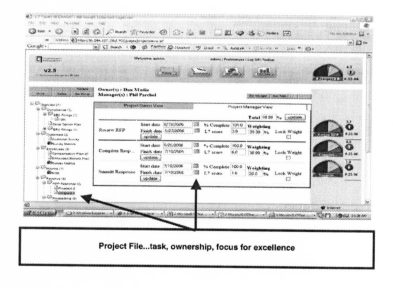

Project File...task, ownership, focus for excellence

The project file view shows the start date and finish date for each project. As mentioned earlier, you provide the initial weighting. As time goes by and deadlines are met (or not), the system adjusts itself based on how well your company is doing against your targets.

Project Files

A Project File is used to track, or update, the status of a project. As such, there are two separate views—one for each of those goals. The simplest way to see the difference between the views is to walk through the process for starting a project.

First, a "Project Owner" will create a new project by selecting a Folder in the Tree Browser, clicking "Add File", giving it a name, selecting "Project" in the pop-up window, and then click "add".

After creating the project, he or she would then click on the new project in the tree browser, and would find themselves in the Project Owner View, below.

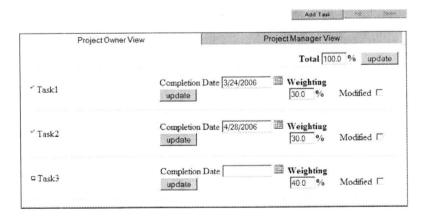

The view shown actually has three tasks already implemented, for clarity, but normally, the window would show up with no tasks. The Project Owner would add one or more tasks by clicking the "Add Task" button at the top of the graphic, and filling in the name.

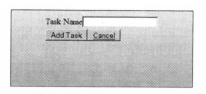

At this point, a Project Manager would normally get involved, by visiting the project and clicking on the "Project Manager View" tab. They would see something like the image below:

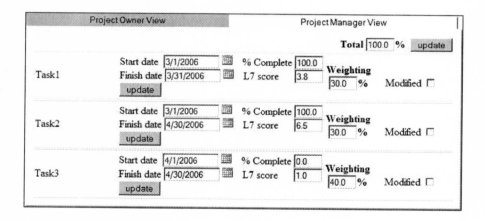

When first viewed, all of the Start and Finish dates will be blank, and the "% Complete" and "L7 Score" fields will be grayed out and inaccessible. The Project Manager starts by entering a Start and Finish date—that is, the dates on which the task is expected to start and finish. Once this is done, he or she can enter a % complete value for that task.

When a % complete value is entered, the L7PMS will automatically calculate an estimated L7 score. This score is based upon the current date, the start and finish dates, and the % complete value the user has entered. Essentially, the L7 score is interpolated from where the project is compared to the percentage of time that has elapsed. On a day that is halfway through the project, one would expect the work to be approximately 50% done. If so, this would equate to an L7 score of 6.0—that is, being on schedule is a 6. One would have to be approximately 20% ahead of schedule to receive a 7.

Of course, the L7PMS cannot know how the difficulty of a task will change over time (the first 50% of the task may be slated to take 75% of the time, for instance …), so the L7 score is overrideable, just by changing the value in the field.

Finishing the Task

At some point, the work has been completed. When this occurs (e.g. when the Project Manager declares the task to be 100% complete), the Project Owner goes to the Project Owner view, and enters the completion date for the appropriate task. **It is this action that "stops the clock."** This is important—for instance, let's assume that the project is 90% complete on the due date. It would likely score a 5.5, because it's behind schedule. A week later, if it's still at 90%, it's further behind schedule, and the L7 score will continue to drop.

The L7 score will continue to drop over time until the Project Owner gives the task a completion date. Until that point, even if it's listed by the Project Manager as 100% complete, the L7 score will continue to drop over time—since from the L7PMS perspective, it's not clear on what date it became 100% complete. The Project Owner must stop the clock and freeze the L7 score by declaring the project "complete."

Re-weighting Tasks

Task weights can be adjusted in the same manner as Folder weights—see the Details View, Re-weighting Folders section above.

Data Files

Data files are used to track hard values (revenue, employee retention, customer satisfaction, cost of labor, etc.) against a target. Individual data points may then be grouped together dynamically.

To add a data, select a folder in the tree browser, click "Add File," give it a name, select "Data File" in the pop-up window, and then click "Add." When the file is created, you can then navigate to it using the tree browser. Upon getting there, you

will see a basically empty page—with the controls to add a data point at the top:

Clicking "Add" and typing in the name of a point (say, "DPoint") will result in a single data point being added. Adding another (say, "DPoint2") will add a second etc., up to a maximum of seven. As with Projects, the weights will automatically distribute evenly, unless you manually change them. After adding two data points, the screen would look about as follows:

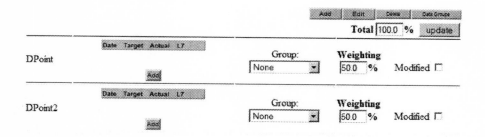

At this point, individual data targets can be entered, via the "Add" button in each row. Clicking "Add" brings up a data box, which lets you enter a target date and value. As an example, let's say we were wanting to track revenue for the year, by quarter. We expect to make $10,000,000 per quarter, with a

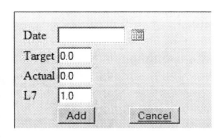

bump at Christmas that will increase December's revenues (and therefore Q4's revenue) by another $5,000,000.

You would enter dates of 4/30, 6/30, 9/30, and 12/31, together with target values of 10, 20, 30, 45, respectively (since it's easiest to just enter the cumulative numbers, not the individual quarterly numbers). After doing this, the page would look something like this the image below:

(Note that the 4th data point is scrolled nearly off the bottom). Note also that the L7 score is 1 (the lowest possible value) on both the target/actual list on the left, and the gauge on the right. That's because the actual value is 0.

Now let's assume that today is April 26th. We made our Q1 mark with about $500,000 left over—so were up by about 5%. If we edit the 3/31 value, and put in 10.5 (our actual revenue in millions), the page will look like this:

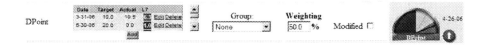

Note that the score has been automatically calculated, and the gauge shows the 6.3 value. This is true even though the other dates are still 1.0—that's because they haven't occurred yet, so the L7PMS knows not to count them yet. So our "DPoint" data point (or Revenue, in this case), is in the green, and will be propagated up as 6.3.

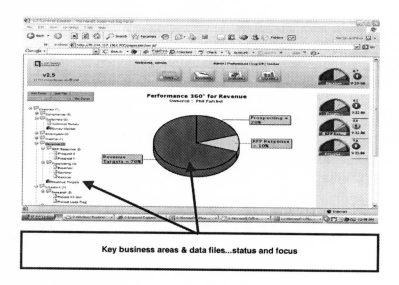

Key business areas & data files...status and focus

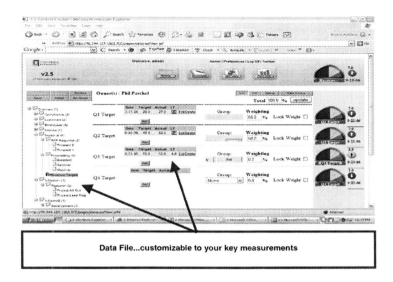

Data File...customizable to your key measurements

Now we will show you a data file.

Another built-in feature of the L7 System is that you determine who has access to information. When you set up the system, you designate who in your organization has access to each file. While the system is designed to be transparent, you might not want to allow company-wide access to each file due to confidentiality issues.

Tree Browser

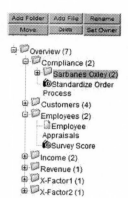

The Tree Browser (at left) allows the user to quickly navigate the hierarchy of their business with a familiar folder view. As the user opens folders and clicks on files, the Folder View (either 360° or Details) will update to reflect the item they have selected.

In addition, the six buttons above the tree allow the user to easily add, rename, move, or delete files and folders, as well as set that element's owner.

An element will have one or more owners—these can be adjusted by selecting owner(s) from the list presented when "Set Owner" is clicked. Note that you can Shift-Click on an owner to select more than one.

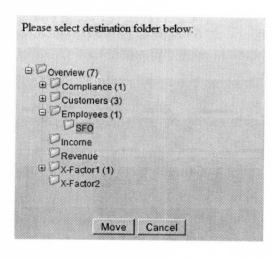

To add a file or folder, select the appropriate button, give the new element a name (and pick whether it's a data or project file, if applicable), and click OK. When moving an element, the application will present the user with another tree (at right), where they can browse to the new location of the element they've selected. Note that you can't move an element onto one of its own children, or ancestors.

Gauges

In any view, the user will see a set of gauges on
the right. These gauges are like the pie slices in
the 360° View—they show the current state of
all of the folder's children. In addition, there is
an "Overview" gauge at the top of the page,
which represents the roll-up of all the gauges—
essentially, the state of the folder you are currently looking at.

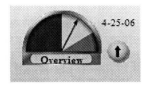

Each gauge has an arrow representing the L7
score (1-7). In addition, the name of the child
("Compliance" or "Customers" in the example
to the right) is shown over a background that
represents the current state of the folder or
file—green (i.e. in the range 6-7), and yellow (in the range 4-6), in the
example to the right.

To the right of each gauge are a trend indicator and a date. The date
indicates the last time that the value of this gauge was changed (presumably by manipulating it directly, or as the result of one of its children
being changed). The trend indicator shows the current state of the
gauge (again, green and yellow in the examples below), together with
the direction of the last change. For the sub-folders "Compliance" the
last changes were positive, and for "Customers," the last changes were
negative.

Top Bar

Every page that is viewed will show a consistent "Top Bar"—the top section of the application. This consists of four elements: the Logo/Version info, the Menu Bar, the Navigation Tiles, and the Summary Gauge. These are explained below.

Logos/Version Info

The L7PMS Logo and version info is at the left edge of the screen. Immediately to the right, if installed, your business logo will be displayed. See the "Logging In" section for an example of a corporate logo being implemented.

Text Bar

The Text Bar consists of two sections: the welcome string, and the action links. The welcome string just shows the User ID of the currently logged-in user. There are four action links, which are detailed here:

Admin

The Admin link will only be visible if the user is an Administrator. If so, then clicking it will take you to a new screen, where you will be able to add and edit users:

UserID	FullName	E-mail	Contact Number	Role			
admin	Level7 Administrator	admin@admin.com	121	SystemAdmin	Edit	Delete	Change Password
John	John Ritz	John@abc.com	3	SystemAdmin	Edit	Delete	Change Password
Bill	Bill Lohan	Bill@abc.com		SystemAdmin	Edit	Delete	Change Password
Taylor	Taylor Binks	taylor@abc.com		SystemAdmin	Edit	Delete	Change Password
Rick	Rick Allen	rick@abc.com		SystemAdmin	Edit	Delete	Change Password
Sue	Sue Wilks	sue@abc.com		SystemAdmin	Edit	Delete	Change Password
Joe	Joe Marshall	joe@abc.com	23	Owner	Edit	Delete	Change Password
Frank	Frank Lebowitz	frank@abc.com		Manager	Edit	Delete	Change Password

Add User

If the "Add User" button (or the "Edit" link for an existing user) is clicked, a pop-up is invoked (as shown below) that allows the user to change personal info about a user, or to grant/revoke privileges.

By navigating the user's tree and selecting the folders that you want to assign privileges to, a user can be allowed to see some folders, own others, and not see others.

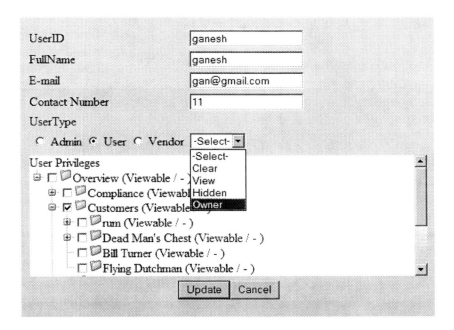

In the example above, the user "ganesh" is being made the Owner of the Customers folder.

User Types: There are three user types: Admin, User, and Vendor. Admins have all rights to view and change data & projects information. Users have all view rights and change rights to their assigned areas. Vendors have no view or change right until an Admin or User grants them rights.

Preferences

Clicking the Preferences link will pop up a window which will allow a user to change their name, email, or contact information, or to change their password.

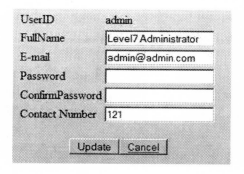

Log Off

Clicking the "Log Off" link will cause the user to be logged out of the L7PMS application. This feature is currently only implemented in Internet Explorer. For other browsers (Firefox, Netscape, Safari, etc.), the user typically has to close the browser window to force the L7PMS to "forget" them.

History

The L7PMS can maintain the history of your organization, so that you can easily track trends. Clicking the "History" tile will pop up a window with a calendar icon. Clicking the calendar icon will result in a view something like the one below.

By selecting a date from the calendar, the user can instruct the system to show the data as it was on that date. For instance, if it were April 26, 2006 (as in the example), and you were preparing a quarterly report for April 30th, you might want to use the calendar to select

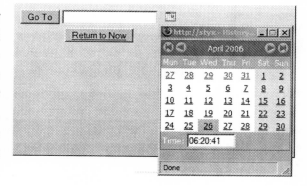

January 1, 2006, so that you could see the state of various initiatives at that point.

Once a date has been selected, the application will continue to display information from that date, even when the user navigates to other folders. This allows for easy analysis across the entire company. To return to the current date, click the History tile again, and select "Return to Now." Any actions that the user takes while in an historical view (adding documents, changing L7 values, etc.) will still be recorded as having happened "today"—no matter what date is being viewed at the time.

Document Storage

The L7PMS will allow users to store and simply revise documents. Documents are attached to a specific folder, so that their context is relevant to their location. Navigating to a folder, and then clicking the Documents tile, will pop up a screen such as the one below:

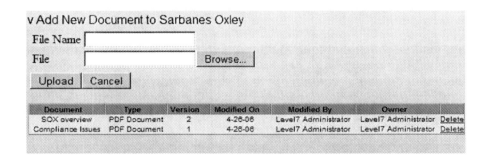

This screen will list the documents that have been attached to this folder. Note that in the example above, there are two: "SOX Overview," and "Compliance Issues." The SOX Overview document has two versions, and the Compliance Issues doc has one. This means that there have been two uploads under the same name—in other words, two revisions of the SOX overview document.

The document titles are hot links that will launch the document in the appropriate application. Clicking on the version number will pop up the version dialog, as shown below:

> Upload New Version

File	Type	Version	Modified On	Modified By	
w9.pdf	PDF Document	1	4-26-06	Level7 Administrator	Delete
w9.pdf	PDF Document	2	4-26-06	Level7 Administrator	Delete

Back

This dialog box allows you to add new versions of a document, or to inspect any previous revision. Versions are automatically numbered, starting at 1, so that if there are *n* versions of a document (as shown in the previous pop up), then the earliest is version 1, and the latest is version *n*.

Detail/360° View

The Detail/360° View Tile allows the user to toggle between the 360° View (i.e., the Pie Chart) and the Details View. These two views are described above, in the "Views" section.

This tile will toggle back and forth from one image to the other, depending on which view the user is in, and which they can switch to. Also, when viewing a file (project or data file), this tile will be "grayed out," since files don't have 360° View "Pie Charts" associated with them.

Print View

Clicking the "Print View" tile will open a "printer friendly" version of the current page in a new window. This version will be missing some of the artifacts that are on the actual page (primarily controls).

A title section will also appear, which will contain the name of the folder (with its path from the top of the tree, or root), the user's name, and the current date. In addition, there is a section labeled "Text," into which the user can type any explanatory information they desire, so that the printed version can be more easily documented.

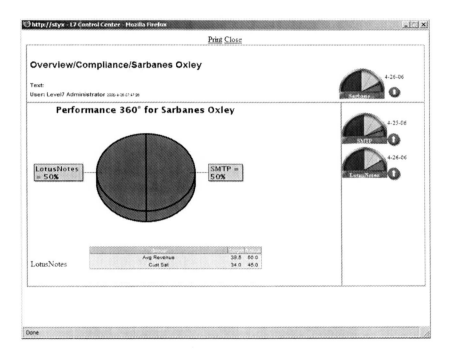

Clicking the "Print" link will pop up your Operating System's "normal" print dialog, allowing the page to be printed.

Summary Gauge

The Summary Gauge is described in the section on Gauges, but just represents the "roll-up" of the element (folder or file) being viewed in the main window. That is, if the user is looking at the Root (top-most folder) with its seven sub-folders, then the Summary Gauge will show the weighted average of the seven sub-folders. It represents the general health of whatever element the user if viewing.

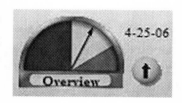

The date and trend-line button, both to the immediate right of the Summary Gauge, show the date that any item that would affect this summary (i.e. is "below" it, or a child of it) changed, and whether that change resulted in an increase or decrease of the L7 score. The color of the button just reflects whether the gauge is currently red (1-4), yellow (4-6), or green (6-7).

The Creators of Level 7 and the L7 Performance Management System are former CEOs, presidents, general managers, and quality leaders who desired to run their business with simplicity and clarity. They have worked for some of the best-managed companies in the world, including General Electric, IBM and BearingPoint, and have built and run several high growth, mid-market companies. The senior team's background includes degrees from MIT, Stamford, and Kellogg, with 70+ years combined experience managing successful growth businesses. The proven concepts behind the L7 Performance Manager™ solution have been successfully deployed and have helped to create clarity, simplicity, and results for business from start-ups to Fortune 500 companies.

The L7 Performance Management Company provides state-of-the-art performance management systems and products focused on helping customers and partners achieve high performance. L7 Performance Management's organizational vision is to greatly advance management performance globally with breakthrough innovations improving our customer's results, and most importantly, improving the lives of our partners and customers. L7 Performance Management is a division of MLG Systems, LLC.

The L7 Performance Management System is a process that aligns strategy and projects with seven universal key business measures. The L7 system provides instant clarity while driving focus for record results … simplified. L7 Performance Management integrates the process of translating strategy into actionable projects, measures, and aligns the business to key company-wide goals. The system is also focused on improving speed and decision quality for businesses through targeting, innovating, and control with increased accountability to maximize results.

For more resources & information, to purchase the L7 Performance Manager for your business, or to explore becoming a Level 7 Consultant or Re-seller Partner call:
203-255-7077 or visit www.L7pm.com

Quotes from L7PMS Users:

One CEO, who has used the Level 7 process to increase revenue at his organization by over 50%, says:

"All of the seven KBMs have the same look and feel, so all the employees can get an instant read on the company's health and help drive results where we need it. It also tells us what areas need attention. My area was behind plan, so it was red. I was confident that with everyone's help, I could make my original plan, so I did not create a new one. The system stores all the plans. This way, we all have a reference point for historical performance to plan."

Other senior managers who have used the Level 7 system say:

"Year after year, most businesses in the second half focus on revenue and cash flow at the expense of having other areas suffer, such as employee and customers, which in the long run negatively impacts revenue and cash flow. The L7 System enables us to look at all the key areas and the impact on revenue and balance them. The system allows us to make plans and it monitors them weekly and daily, so we can make changes to our focus faster than our competitors."

"The L7 System has taken the burden off of me and made us all focused on the key areas. It has relieved stress and tension and has focused people in areas that they are best suited for and where they can contribute the most."

"Having our key focus areas and projects recorded in the system make it easy to update and track, to make sure we are achieving the results that we need, when we need them."

"It allows us to quickly see where we are today relative to our goals and key projects. We can see where we will end up and make changes to the strategy and programs."

"With the L7 system we now have a central system with names and dates to ensure ownership and execution."

"The L7 system is very intuitive. It supports our existing management philosophy and business process, and does not try to recreate it all."

"L7 is very flexible ... the system adapts to us, not us having to adapt to the system."

"The business managers are on the same page with key goals and programs and are in agreement ... everyone is on the same page, and it shows in our results."

About the Authors

Michael Goolden is President and CEO of L7 Performance Management.

Michael spent over 20 years in successively responsible positions with the General Electric Company. After graduating from GE's Financial Services Management Development Program and executing several successful years in both sales and sales management, he served in diverse executive management roles and various business segments. Michael's positions included Senior Vice President and Region Manager, Vice President of Global Six Sigma Quality, and General Manager and President. Michael's teams and businesses consistently produced record growth results. He holds a Bachelor of Science degree in Business Management from Ithaca College and a Masters in Management from Northwestern University's Kellogg Graduate School of Business. Michael lives in Connecticut with his wife and three children.

Sandra Goolden is a writer and project manager who has raised millions of dollars for her clients by writing dozens of successful proposals to government agencies and private foundations. She holds a B.A. from St. Lawrence University and a Masters in Public Administration from SUNY's Rockefeller College of Public Affairs. She resides on an island in Maine with her young son.

978-0-595-44502-8
0-595-44502-0